Electric Cars, Bikes, Vans

written by Jeff Allan
illustrated by Maddie Cottam-Allan

DEDICATION

for
Professor Sir David McKay [1]
whose book "Sustainable Energy - without the hot air"
was my inspiration for this book.

[1] Sir David John Cameron MacKay (22 April 1967 – 14 April 2016) was a British physicist, mathematician, and academic. He was the Regius Professor of Engineering in the Department of Engineering at the University of Cambridge and from 2009 to 2014 was Chief Scientific Advisor to the UK Department of Energy and Climate Change

Electric Cars, Bikes, Vans and Trucks

CONTENTS

Electric Cars, Bikes, Vans and Trucks

ACKNOWLEDGEMENTS

Thanks to my family - Amanda, Jenny, Ben, Jamie and Maddie for putting up with my obsession with electric cars and hydrogen trains.

I am most grateful to my mentor Professor Brian Mellitt for kindling my interest in electric traction.

I am indebted to Maddie who has simultaneously brought humour and art to the book.

Thanks also to the many people who, largely by means of social media, have contributed to my knowledge. They are too numerous to mention but I must except Lynne Woolliscroft whose advice on economics deserves special acknowledgement and Steve Hunter for our discussion on battery electric versus fuel cell trucks.

I am grateful for proof/beta-reading carried out by Penny Harrison.

Lastly, I would like to thank Royal Pavilion & Museums, Brighton and Hove for permission to use the copy of the photograph of Magnus Volk to be found on page 72, Kerbocharge for the photo on page 43 and ULEMCo for the photo on page 68.

Electric Cars, Bikes, Vans and Trucks

1 INTRODUCTION

Electric cars, bikes, vans and trucks have electric motors and batteries.

They may depend solely on the battery (in the case of battery electric cars, vans or trucks).

They may include a petrol or diesel engine (in the case of hybrid cars or vans).

They may include a hydrogen fuel cell (in the case of hydrogen fuel cell cars or trucks)

Or, in the case of electric bikes, they may include human pedal power.

The first 14 chapters of this edition focus on battery electric cars, hybrid cars and hydrogen fuel cell cars, followed by electric bikes, vans - battery electric and hybrid and trucks - hydrogen fuel cell and battery electric.
There are then chapters on converting petrol cars, history, future trends and amateur car motor sport.

The chapter *"Getting Further Information"* includes links evidencing statements and providing information on the contents of all preceding chapters.

This edition also includes an index of words or phrases and associated pointers ('locators') to where useful material can be found in the book and closes with some information about the author and illustrator.

I started writing this book in 2016. It has been updated regularly and this 10th edition (2025) has been significantly expanded. Much has changed since 2016 - there is a much better understanding by the general public for the need to do something about emissions to halt or preferably reverse climate change. This is in no small measure due to heroes such as the Swedish environmental activist Greta Thunberg. The youth of today are taking the lead in pointing out the need for action.

Changing from a diesel or petrol car to a battery electric (or hybrid) undoubtedly reduces emissions but you can reduce them still further. This is explained in the chapter *"Are You Saving the Planet?"*.

The government has set a target of 2030 for the elimination of new petrol or diesel cars in the UK. It may surprise readers that progress since 2016 is on target in 2025. (See *"Getting Further Information"* chapter).

Now it is time to start reading the book! You do not have to read it sequentially, although as I have explained I have tried to provide the information in a helpful and logical order; nor do you have to read every word of every chapter! However you choose to do it, if you are reading this book, you have a pioneering spirit. If you drive an electric car you are a pioneer.

2 THE PROS AND CONS OF BATTERY ELECTRIC CARS

It takes a while but gradually you realise how awful a petrol or diesel car is. The first thing you notice in a battery electric car is that there is no engine to start. You do not have to worry about the car stalling. Unlike a car with a manual gearbox car, there is no clutch, just "Park" and two directions – "Forward (Drive) "and "Reverse". For those of you who are used to driving an automatic car which may seem to be similar, there is even a difference here. An automatic still has multiple gears and you will know when it changes gear because there is a slight change in acceleration and you will see the RPM of the engine change. A battery electric car is capable of going from zero speed to top speed in one go, without the need to change gears (in the case of my Tesla, from 0 to a top speed, which is limited to 155mph). Many battery electric cars have one pedal operation with acceleration reduced then braking applied as the accelerator is eased off.

There are more benefits. The car is extremely quiet. So quiet, indeed, that manufacturers of new battery electric cars have added a noise at low speeds to warn unwary pedestrians. The car is clean. It is amazing how much smell there is when filling a petrol or diesel car with fuel. Some will be surprised to find that avoiding the need to fill up at a petrol station is a benefit. What about the problem of charging a battery electric car? There is more detail later but for most people, it is possible to charge effortlessly at home or work while the car is not being used.

The battery is heavy but placed very low down. This makes an electric car particularly stable when cornering.

When you take your foot off the accelerator, it will slow the car down, like a petrol or diesel car in a low gear. Unlike a petrol or diesel car a battery electric car also uses the energy needed to slow it down to recharge the battery! When you press the brake, even more energy is fed into the battery. This means less wear on the brakes (and therefore lower maintenance costs) and you are saving energy.

If you want the heating or air conditioning on while you are stationary, there is no need to worry about polluting the air nearby as you would with a petrol or diesel car. if you find yourself stuck in a long traffic jam, don't worry about running out of battery due to the heating or air conditioning. A battery will be able to power these for many hours with little reduction in battery capacity. N.B. as is the case in many modern petrol or diesel engines, battery electric cars stop the motor when the car is stationary.

Most electric cars are safer in an accident than their equivalent petrol or diesel equivalent. This is explained further in the "Safety" Chapter.

In winter, many electric cars are capable of defrosting the car before you drive without you having to be in the car. Similarly, they can cool the car before you drive. An internal combustion engine car would need you to be in the car while the cabin is made comfortable or risk having your car stolen.

So, are there any disadvantages?
If you have to drive a long distance, then you may need to charge the car part way through the journey. If your electric car has limited range this can increase the journey time significantly but if you have a battery electric car with a good range, for example a Tesla, this break in driving is likely to be needed in any case to refresh the driver as well as the car.

Most people do not notice that a petrol or diesel car uses more fuel in the winter than the summer. The difference with a battery electric car is more marked. You may easily have less than 2/3 of the range in winter than you have in summer. As long as you bear this in mind when selecting your electric car, this should not be a problem but it does catch out a number of new drivers of electric cars.

In the UK you will still be one of a relatively few people driving a battery electric car. In Norway close to 100% of cars are now battery electric cars and, at the time of writing, over 19% of new cars in the UK are battery electric. Electric cars are getting more popular in the UK. It is difficult to move more than a few hundred yards in a large city without spotting a battery electric car. You can tell whether a car is battery electric because it has no exhaust pipes and may have a green band on the number plates.

3 ASSESSING YOUR NEEDS, IF A BATTERY ELECTRIC CAR IS FOR YOU

Size of the boot, number of seats, height, length, width, colour, price are all familiar factors that are considered when choosing a petrol or diesel car, whether new or used. There are other similar factors that may be considered and these all apply equally to battery electric cars. It is rare that the size of the fuel tank for a petrol or diesel car is a consideration but for a battery electric car, range is a consideration uppermost in most people's minds. It is not a good idea to select a battery electric car solely on range considerations, though. A small battery electric car with a great range for example may not be the best choice for a large family.

How can you determine what range you do need and whether a low range is adequate for your needs? If you drive a petrol or diesel car at present, one effective way is to use the phone app EV8 Switch which is available for android phones and iPhone phones obtainable from wherever you normally get your apps (for example app store for iPhones). After you have installed the EV8 app, it will automatically monitor your travel by petrol or diesel car and provide reports as shown below.

The report below shows daily journeys - where you have been, the start time, mileage and average speed. You can delete individual journeys. For example, it may pick up a bus journey, a train journey or a car journey where you are being driven rather than driving your own car or using another person's car.

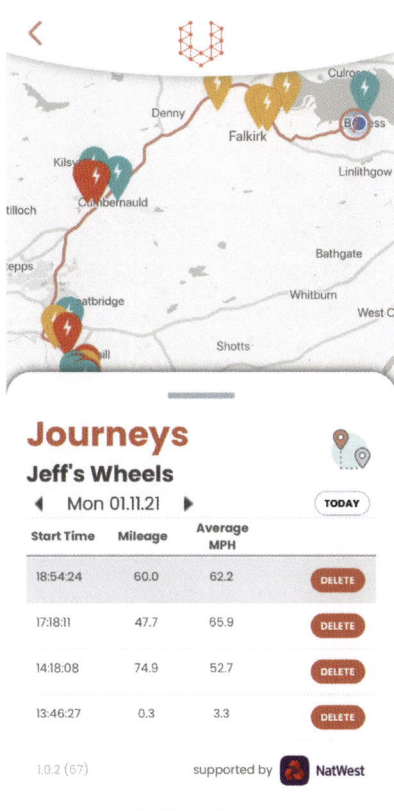

Report on daily journeys

Another report shows the total mileage monitored, the average weekly miles, the average daily miles and the number of days that data has been collected. It also shows data for individual days and whether a short range, medium range or long range EV would be suitable. For most people, even those making the occasional long journey, a short range EV is usually adequate, although for a long journey it is necessary to charge during the journey (See *"Driving Long Distances"* chapter).

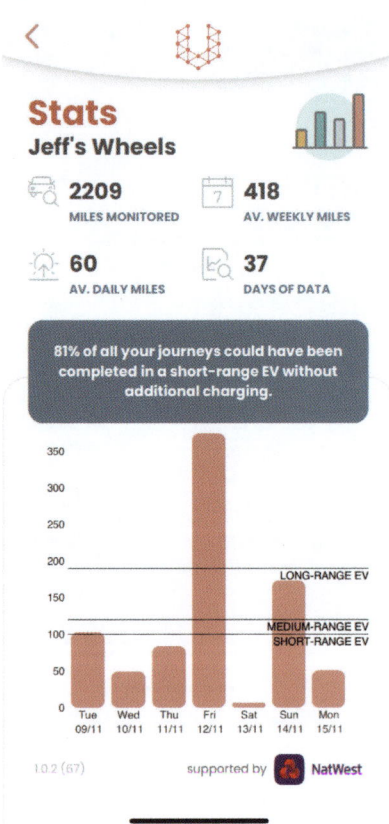

Report on total journeys

Once you have established whether you need a short range, medium range or long range car, the app shows new cars available that meet these needs. An example of short range cars is shown below.

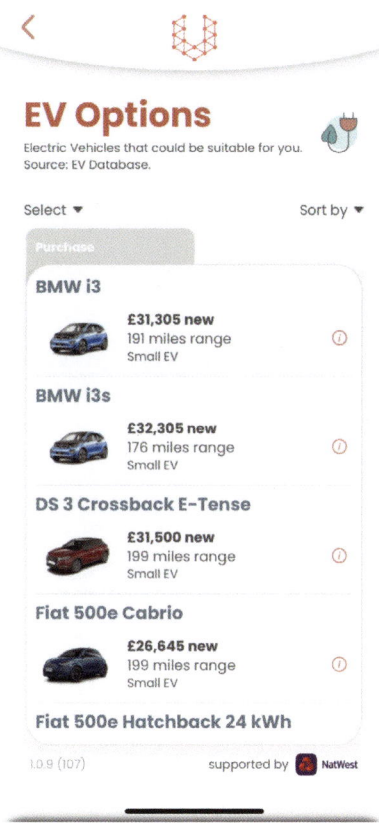

Report on new cars available

The report shown below gives examples of journey types and how switching to a battery electric car would reduce emissions.

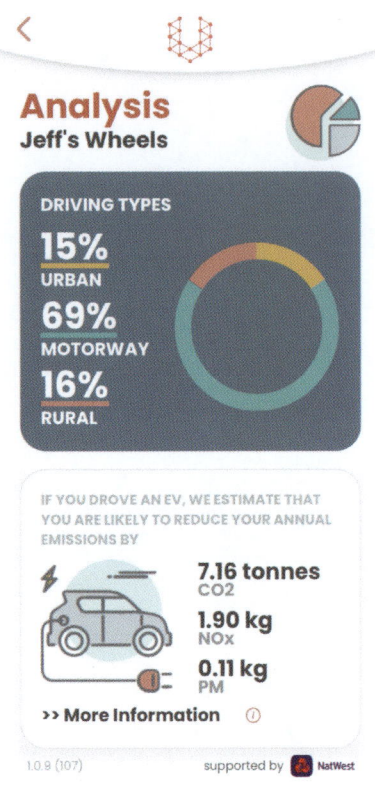

Report on emissions

If you are going to buy a new or used electric car you also need to consider charging at home (See *"Charging at Home"* chapter).

4 ECONOMICS

It will surprise many readers of this book to find that running a battery electric car is usually cheaper than running an equivalent petrol or diesel car. You need to take into account all the costs of running a car : Initial cost of car minus final sale price of your car, or leasing cost , installing home charging (where applicable), charging costs , depreciation , fuel costs , vehicle tax cost, Benefit In Kind (BIK) cost (where applicable), insurance cost, servicing cost, MOT cost (where applicable), interest on any loan needed for your car, congestion charge (where applicable), low emission area charge (where applicable). All prices in this book are referenced to December 2024.

Let's consider each in turn, starting with **capital or leasing costs.** If you buy your car, whether new or used, you need to consider the up-front capital cost. Battery electric cars generally incur a higher up-front cost than an equivalent petrol or diesel car but this price difference is decreasing and in the case of the Vauxhall Frontera, for example, has reached parity.

If you live in a flat, you can get a grant of up to £350 to have a **home charger** installed and this applies to a new car or a used car. Some manufacturers offer to install a home charger as part of the deal of buying a battery electric car. (See *"Getting Further Information"* chapter).

Battery electric cars used to depreciate appreciably but now it is usual to find that battery electric cars depreciate less than their petrol or diesel car equivalent, so you may find the difference between the price you paid at the beginning of ownership and the sale price at the end is less than for a petrol or diesel car. With regard to **leasing** costs, these are a little higher for battery electric cars, but as time goes by, less so.

I would like to give a practical example to demonstrate **fuel costs.** I drive a Tesla Model S. I have therefore chosen an equivalent petrol car - a Jaguar XF to provide a comparison. My annual mileage is around 10,000 miles. I know that my Tesla consumes 0.361kWh (kilowatt-hour) per mile. My electricity bill shows that I pay £0.227 per kWh. Therefore, if I charged my car fully at home, it would cost £10,000*0.361*0.227 = £819.47. In fact, I often charge at Tesla superchargers for long journeys. These are free for me as my Tesla was one of the first and free supercharging was provided for the life of the car! Another factor is that I have solar cells on the roof of my house so in practice, my fuel costs are a fraction of the above amount.

Now consider the equivalent petrol car. A Jaguar XF with a 3 litre engine has a fuel consumption of up to 27 miles per gallon on economy combined city and open road use. A litre of petrol costs about £1.37 today and there are 4.6 litres per gallon. An annual mileage of 10,000 would, therefore, cost £10,000*1.37*4.6/27 = £2334.07.

With regard to **vehicle tax,** my Tesla Model S currently has zero vehicle tax, although it must be taxed every year. A Jaguar XF, of a similar age, would be charged £745.50 per year. Vehicle tax for petrol or electric cars varies according to the type of car but generally the vehicle tax for a battery electric car will either be zero or less than for an equivalent petrol car. Vehicle tax for alternative fuel vehicles including hybrids is not zero after year one but are less than for petrol/diesel equivalents.

Benefit in Kind (BIK) applies to when a car is provided as part of your work as a benefit. This is the tax which you pay for that benefit. BIK rates are complicated to work out but generally speaking, battery electric cars attract lower BIK rates.

Insurance costs are broadly similar for all engine types.

Servicing costs are lower for battery electric cars because there are fewer moving parts. Despite having driven over 100,000 miles in my Tesla, it still has the original brake pads and discs. Interestingly, I used to have my Tesla serviced once per year but when I contacted my Tesla dealer recently, I was told they don't bother with an annual service and instead just fix things when they go wrong!

The cost of a **MOT** test is the same for all cars, regardless of engine type.

Interest on loans is not affected by the engine type, although it will vary considerably dependent on where you get your loan.

Battery electric cars qualify for a 100% discount from the **congestion charge** in London but you have to register for that exemption and there is a registration fee of £10 each year. The exemption is expected to be withdrawn in December 2025. (See *"Getting Further Information"* chapter).

Battery electric cars qualify for the 100% cleaner vehicle discount in the London Ultra Low Emission Zone at present but it is advisable to check if you plan to drive in London regularly. Other UK cities now operate Low Emission Zones (LEZ) or Clean Air Zones (CAZ) which may offer exemptions or discounts for vehicles with zero or very low emissions. If you intend to travel to e.g. Birmingham, Bristol, Oxford, Bath, Bradford, Portsmouth, Newcastle / Gateshead, Sheffield, Southampton, Aberdeen, Dundee, Edinburgh or Glasgow (list correct at the time of writing) you may wish to check this out.

So far, the costs I have described are personal costs but there are costs to society associated with driving a car, whether battery electric, diesel or petrol in terms of effect on climate change, the planet's limited resources and harm to health of the general public. These are covered in the next chapter *"Are You Saving the Planet?"*.

In summary, fuel costs, vehicle tax, BIK, servicing costs, congestion charge London Ultra Low Emission Zone and LEZ/CAZ costs are either zero or much lower for a battery electric car than a petrol or diesel car. Capital costs may be higher for a battery electric car but depreciation may be less. Individual cases need to be considered but generally the running costs of a battery electric car should be cheaper than the equivalent petrol or diesel car.

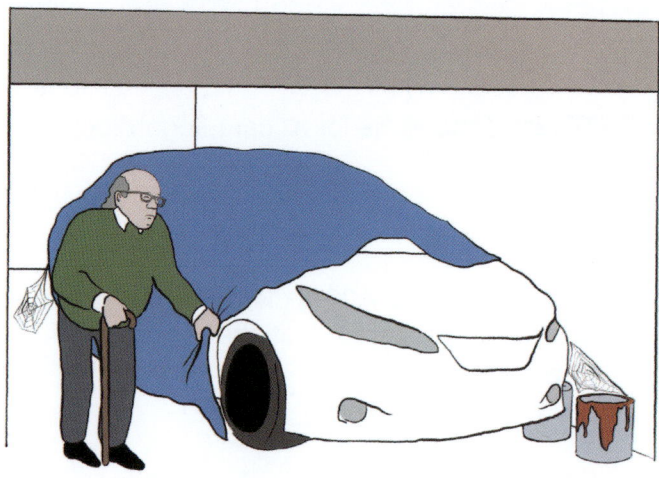

5 LIFETIME CONSIDERATIONS

The good news is that there is no clutch or gearbox to wear out. Furthermore, the electric motors and controlling electric system (power electronics) used in electric cars are considerably more robust than petrol or diesel engines. They are likely to outlive the rest of the car. Brake wear is less than on other types of car too because electric cars have a regenerative brake. This means that (as mentioned previously) the electric motor in a battery electric car acts like a brake when the foot is taken off the accelerator and also (for some cars) when the foot is placed on the brake. The energy produced is fed into the battery slightly extending the range. This electric braking action means conventional brake pads and discs last longer. My electric car shows little sign of brake pad or disc wear in over 100,000 miles of use.

The bad news is that the large weight of the battery typically means that battery electric and hybrid cars are heavier than an equivalent petrol or diesel equivalent and therefore tyre wear may be more (but not significantly more).

If anything does go wrong with the motor or battery, replacement can be expensive. The need for replacement is unlikely, unless associated with accident damage. Other than in this case, the motor is likely to last much longer than the equivalent for a petrol or diesel car. This is because there are fewer moving parts (there are no pistons, crankshafts, gearbox, camshafts, injectors etc.). The only wear in a battery electric motor is on the bearings, but even this is much less than the wear on the bearings in a petrol or diesel engine. There is no gearbox but there is a reduction drive. The reduction drive, because it is constantly engaged, is not under the same stress as a variable speed gearbox that would be found on a petrol or diesel car. The reduction drive is likely to outlive the rest of the car.

Due to the high level of taxation on petrol and diesel oil, fuel (electricity) costs should be less. This may not be the case if you are dependent on charging stations away from home on a frequent basis if you have to pay a fee to use them. (See *"Economics"* chapter).

Battery life is difficult to predict. Over a long period of time, batteries deteriorate. As a result, the range reduces, but it is for the car owner to decide when a battery needs replacing - If the owner is willing to tolerate a reduced range, then the battery can continue to be used. One driver may feel the need to replace a battery with a reduced range of 90% compared to the range for a new car. Another driver may be willing to allow it to reduce to say 70% before replacement. Eventually a battery will expire, but not without warning of considerably reduced range. Battery life is typically measured in full cycles i.e. charging to 100% and discharging to 0%. One battery manufacturer quotes 1500 full cycles. (A full cycle is where you charge to 100% then discharge to 0%). This seems to be an alarmingly small number. However electric car manufacturers typically prevent drivers from discharging to 0% and some prevent charging to 100%. This extends the number of cycles that can be used considerably. I would estimate that 1500 cycles could easily correspond to 200,000 miles if care is taken. There are a number of actions which a driver can take to extend battery life.

These include:

(As for any rechargeable battery)
1. Do not leave the car at full charge for any lengthy period. (Most electric cars have a facility to charge it to a particular % - 80% is a good figure to charge it to, if you are leaving it for a while).
2. Charge the car before it has fallen below 20%.
3. Do not leave the battery for extended periods of time in a state of low charge.
and
4. Charge at home or work (or both) whenever possible rather than charging routinely at the higher rate obtainable from high speed chargers. This is because charging regularly at the higher rate may shorten the life of the battery due to the extra stress placed on it while charging at this rate.

However, there will be times when you need a full charge and you may find your journey forces you to use the battery until the charge is less than 20%. Occasional use is not a problem.

To give some indication of a typical time period for the life of a battery, when I bought my Tesla, the battery was guaranteed for eight years (with unlimited mileage). Battery prices are falling over time so by the time you need a new battery, in perhaps 15 years, or more, the price of a replacement battery should be much less than the original cost.

6 SAFETY

It may be surprising to learn that most battery electric cars are safer than the equivalent petrol or diesel car. Even more surprisingly this is due to the battery. The battery is a structural part of the car and strengthens the car providing better protection in a crash than an equivalent petrol or diesel car. The Tesla model S was the first car to achieve 5 stars in European NCAP safety ratings. The tests have got stricter since then but Tesla consistently scores 5 stars (See *"Getting Further Information"* chapter).

Although a battery electric car has the potential to give a lethal electric shock, there are many safety features which prevent this from happening. It is for example perfectly safe to charge your car while it is raining. Nevertheless, it is advisable not to use a high-pressure hose to clean your car when it is charging.

To ensure this inherent safety, a home charger should be installed by an electrician qualified to fit electric chargers. Cables should also be replaced if they have suffered physical damage.

Fires in electric cars receive far more, and unfair, press attention than fires in petrol or diesel cars, even though they are far less likely to occur. Fires in either type of car are dangerous for different reasons. If you suspect a fire while in a car, maybe due to a burning smell, smoke or worse still flames, the advice is the same - leave the car immediately and move a safe distance away before calling the emergency fire service. A fire in a petrol car is likely to lead to an explosion once the fire reaches the petrol tank.

A fire in a battery electric car is different. You need fuel, oxygen and an ignition source for a fire. The problem with a battery fire in a battery electric car is that it is likely to produce a continuous ignition source if the battery is damaged. The fire service may have to monitor a battery electric car for up to 24 hours after putting the fire out for that reason (See *"Getting Further Information"* chapter).

Safety considerations for hydrogen fuel cell cars are different and are covered in the *"Hydrogen Fuel Cell Cars"* chapter.

7 ARE YOU SAVING THE PLANET?

If you want to save the planet, don't buy a car, not even a battery electric car - walk instead. If you need to travel further, use a bicycle (See *"Electric Bikes"* chapter). If you need to go further still, use a sustainable form of public transport, for example a full or substantially full electric train powered from renewable sources such as wind, hydro, solar or nuclear. (See *"Getting Further Information"* chapter).

However, for some, a car is essential, particularly for those with reduced mobility or living in rural areas or those not well served by public transport. Furthermore, many, like selfish me, cannot resist the luxury and enjoyment of a car. A better question may be "Are you treating the planet better by using a battery electric or hybrid car rather than a petrol, diesel or even a hydrogen fuel cell powered car?" The simple answer is YES, but it is a complex issue which I will try to explain. There are people who will say 'no' but these are all too often people who have a vested interest in exploiting fossil fuels or current automotive technology.

One important point if you live in a city is that you are saving lives by driving a battery electric car rather than a petrol or diesel car because there are no carcinogenic tail pipe emissions. It is a sobering thought that nearly 40,000 people a year die an early death from air pollution in the UK. Contrast this with less than 2000 deaths per year from road accidents in the UK. See *"Getting Further Information"* chapter for more information on this.

Let us get back to the question - *"Are You Saving the Planet?"*. There are two elements to consider - emissions (especially carbon dioxide), and material resources. It is necessary also to consider the manufacture of the car, the use of the car and the disposal of the car - so called cradle to grave. Let us start with energy.

Energy is needed to extract the raw materials to make any car, namely to transport the raw materials to the factory, to manufacture a car, to transport a car to the dealer, to prepare a car for a new owner, to deliver a car to a new owner. All this energy is needed before an owner of a new car has driven the first mile. Volkswagen claim to achieve net zero on car production but for other manufacturers, this energy may not be solely from renewable resources. Some emissions, chiefly carbon dioxide but also others will have been produced. How much energy is needed? Does a battery electric car need more energy for these processes?

Consider the vehicle part manufacturing and assembly process. This is where the majority of the energy to manufacture (and scrap) a car is used. It takes around 9400 kilowatt hours (kWh) of energy to turn raw materials into a finished petrol or diesel car. A battery electric car needs up to 50% more energy due to the manufacturing of the battery - around 14000kWh, but these figures need to be considered in the whole lifecycle and are reducing all the time. The figure given here is a conservative, high value. The energy of 14000kWh would be enough to power my electric car for 40,000 miles. The energy used to run my electric car for a lifetime of 100,000 miles would therefore be just over 2.5 times the energy to manufacture it. In other words, the increased energy to manufacture a battery electric rather than a petrol or diesel car is significant. This means that for a battery electric car to be better than a petrol car or a diesel car in terms of carbon dioxide emissions, the generation of electricity used to run a battery electric car must produce less carbon dioxide emission than that produced when running a petrol or diesel car. However most electric cars have a lifetime much longer than 100,000 miles.

I am hoping for 300,000 from mine over 30 years. *(See "Getting Further Information"* chapter).

The carbon dioxide emissions for a battery electric car are dependent on the fuel mix of the electricity generation. In Norway, for example, virtually 100% of the electricity is produced from renewable sources - mainly hydro-electric generation, thus close to zero carbon dioxide emissions are produced when driving a battery electric car in Norway. Due to the high volume of electricity produced from nuclear power in France, train journeys within that country produce little in the way of carbon dioxide emission. At the other extreme, in China, at present, a large percentage of the electricity is produced from coal which produces large quantities of carbon dioxide. In fact, and this is a most significant fact, if your electricity is generated by coal, you may produce less carbon dioxide by driving a smaller petrol or diesel car than a battery electric car! If you are reading this in China, please still consider buying a battery electric car for two reasons - firstly your car will not produce tail pipe emissions which will clog the atmosphere in your city, secondly China is rapidly changing the fuel mix of electricity, reducing the need for coal and increasing the use of renewable fuels to replace dependency on coal. The same can be said at the time of writing for USA, India, Japan and South Korea. The UK mix is improving rapidly too - In 2024, over 50% of UK power came from renewables. After 30th September 2024, Britain had no coal-fired power generation on its grid effectively without coal for the first time since the Industrial Revolution. You can find information on the UK daily mix, the effect of changing the mix and the annual fuel mix for each nation. (See *"Getting Further Information"* chapter).

Consider this simple calculation. My Tesla has required an average of 354 Watt-hours of electricity per mile in the last ten years/ 126,000 miles. As I write, the national grid is producing 127 grammes of carbon dioxide per kilo-Watt hour. Therefore, my car will produce 127 multiplied by .354 grammes of carbon dioxide per mile, which is 45 grammes of carbon dioxide per mile if I power it from the national grid. My Tesla is a fast, 2 tonne, comfortable 5-seater car. For comparison, a similar size diesel Jaguar car, a 3 litre turbo charged XJ Luxury produces nearly 300 grammes of carbon dioxide per mile. Note that if it had been a petrol rather than diesel engine it would produce even more carbon dioxide.

Smaller petrol or diesel cars produce less carbon dioxide but equally so do smaller electric cars run on national grid electricity.

In the UK, based on present electricity generation fuel mix, use of a battery electric car will produce less carbon dioxide and associated emissions than an equivalent petrol or diesel car, providing the car is used for a reasonable lifetime (in excess of around 50,000 miles) before being scrapped.

You can improve the situation further by fitting solar cells to your house roof - my solar cells have produced more energy than I have used in my car. If I ran my car exclusively from the energy produced from my solar cells, the car would release no carbon dioxide during use.

There are other emissions. Battery electric and hybrid cars tend to be heavier than petrol or diesel cars so tyre wear is greater. However, the electric brake systems in battery electric and hybrid cars means that they produce less brake dust than petrol or diesel cars. The issue of tyre and brake emissions is a serious one for city dwellers in particular. Electric cars are approximately similar to petrol and diesel cars in this area and it is to be expected that this remaining significant health problem will need to be addressed, even if we all eliminate tail pipe emissions by changing over to electric cars. (See *"Getting Further Information"* chapter).

Let us now turn our attention to the use of material resources. In the early 1950s, cars were predominantly made of steel, with a small amount of aluminium, rubber and Bakelite (an early form of plastic). Cars now, whether petrol, diesel, hybrid or battery electric utilise more exotic materials - platinum, for example is used in catalytic converters for petrol cars. More aluminium is used to reduce body weight and plastics abound. The numerous electric motors in a petrol car for heating and ventilation, windscreen wipers, starter motors, electric seats and tailgates utilise other resources such as copper and magnetic materials which a battery electric car will typically use in even greater quantities for the motors that drive the wheels. This is before the extra resources in batteries are considered. If our planet is not to be denuded by the production and use of cars, then recycling at the end of car life is paramount. Recycling of steel has been dealt with for some time.

Recycling of rarer materials is also being resolved. (See *"Getting Further Information"* chapter).

Recycling of electric car batteries can begin by electricity companies utilising remaining electric storage capabilities. This needs further explanation. When electricity is generated for domestic use, it has to be used at the time of generation because of costs and problems of traditional methods of storage such as pumped water. A used electric car battery will have diminished range for the electric car but may still be used together with other used car batteries by electricity utilities to store solar electricity generated during the day and released from the used car batteries in the hours of darkness when people want to cook, heat and light their homes. A used electric car battery can be given a second life before being taken apart for recycling its constituent parts. (See *"Getting Further Information"* chapter).

At the beginning of the chapter a hydrogen powered car was mentioned. A hydrogen powered car using a fuel cell (which converts hydrogen into electricity) produces no tail pipe emissions, but presently has less than half the efficiency of a battery powered electric car.

There is interest in this technology as a replacement for diesel engines in the area of trucks and railway engines where the reduced efficiency compared to battery in electric trucks and railway trains is tolerated due to the short range, heavy weight and high cost of battery electric alternatives. Battery technology is catching up fast and we are already seeing battery electric trucks.

In conclusion, in the UK, a battery electric car will produce less carbon dioxide emissions than an equivalent petrol or diesel car providing it is used for a reasonable lifetime mileage to offset the increased energy needed to produce it. Emissions other than tail pipe emissions (tyre and brake dust) are as much of a problem with battery electric cars as with petrol or diesel cars and remain a health concern. The increased use of more exotic resources than steel in modern car design, particularly those in electric cars needs particular attention to recycling at the end of life. In other countries the calculation will be different, depending upon the sources of electricity in that country (as per Norway /China, referenced above.)

8 BUYING OR LEASING A NEW CAR

The advantage of buying or leasing a new electric car rather than a used electric car is that you will benefit from the latest technology. This can be important as the technology is changing fast, particularly the available range and driver automation.

The question most often put to drivers of electric cars is "What is the range?". The time is coming when that question will not need to be asked. It is rarely asked about a petrol or diesel car and it is a difficult question to answer.

Standards are useful to compare one car manufacturer with another but are not always indicative of the type of range you might achieve practically. The most recent standard WLTP (Worldwide harmonised Light vehicle Test Procedure) is supposed to reflect realistic ranges. Unfortunately, some car manufacturers are getting wise to these standards and there have been reports of some dubious values being quoted by manufacturers.

Range is dependent on temperature, speed, type of use and will therefore vary from driver to driver and time of year. The effect of temperature is considerable. People who buy electric cars are often disappointed at the very noticeable reduction in range when the weather gets cold. It is not unusual to experience a 30%

reduction in range in freezing temperatures compared to a summer 's day. There are several reasons for this - the battery is less efficient in cold temperatures and there is typically the extra burden of heating which can be a drain on the battery.

Ideally most owners would like to buy a battery electric car which can be charged when not being used, typically overnight at home and have sufficient range to complete all the driving required during the day or even better for several days. If this can be achieved, this is better than a diesel or petrol car as you will not have the inconvenience and the expense of filling up at a fuel service station. If you have a long commute for example, it may be useful to also charge at work. Increasingly, workplaces provide the means to charge during work time. If you have a very long commute, say in excess of 200 miles, you may charge on the way at a high speed public charging point. This could take 30 minutes or less but may provide a useful break to driving, particularly as these are typically located at service stations or other similar amenities.

The best way to find out what is involved in living with a particular new car is to try it out for a day, preferably a few days, to see what is involved. If it is your first electric car you may not have a home charging facility but it may be possible to charge it slowly from a domestic socket or to get the dealer to charge it fully before handing it over for your trial.

The best time to try it out is in winter as range decreases significantly in cold weather. If the range is sufficient for you in cold weather it will be more than sufficient in the warm weather. If you can only try it in the summer, then as a rough guide assume your range may be a third less in the winter.

Another point to consider with range is that even if the car will suit your everyday needs, you will also have to consider its use for occasional longer journeys. If you want to go for a very long drive and charge on the way at a public charging point, you may need to download an app or apply for a charge card in advance or borrow one from the dealer. (See *Driving Long Distances"* chapter). The reason for this is that while some public charge points accept credit or debit cards at present, not all do. Your journey time will be extended compared to a petrol or diesel car if you need to charge on a longer journey. Even if you rarely travel on a long journey, it is worth trying out a long journey on your trial.

If you make frequent long journeys an additional consideration other than range is the speed at which the car can be charged - a typical measure is the time to charge from 20% to 80% of battery capacity (effectively range). Note the last 20% from 80% to 100% takes much longer than the previous 20% of charging.

Availability of high speed chargers is important for frequent long journeys. The Tesla supercharger network has been consistently the best in the UK and mainland Europe. Tesla cars still have full use of the extensive Tesla supercharger network available throughout Europe so this can be an advantage. Some Tesla superchargers are made accessible to other makes, but not all parts of the network are available. Download the Tesla app to your phone to use these chargers and see which are available for other makes of car.

Tesla Superchargers being used by other makes e.g. Audi

There is now a wide variety of battery electric cars available - more than 130 models in 2025. Virtually every car manufacturer has a battery electric car product.

The following give some idea of the variety of new battery electric cars you can buy or lease.

The vehicle below is not strictly a car but a quadricycle. it is very cheap and very slow - 28mph maximum speed and it is not allowed on motorways.

Citroën AMI

One of the cheapest battery electric cars in 2025 has won the Car of Year Award - the Renault 5 battery electric.

Another alternative is the BYD Dolphin, a practical small car manufactured by the largest battery electric car manufacturer in the world. The Chinese make BYD took over the number one slot in annual production of battery electric cars from Tesla in 2024 - a total of more than 1.7million battery electric cars. The Dolphin packs many features in one of the lowest costs for a battery car.

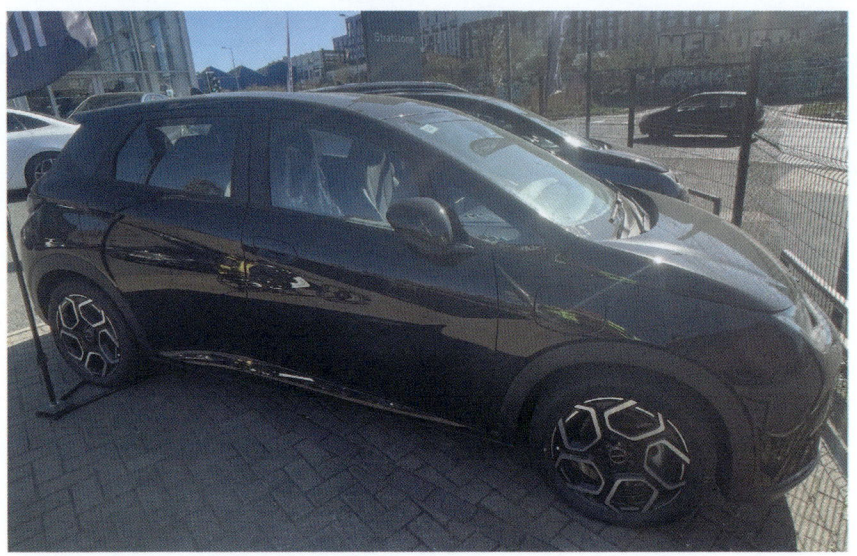

BYD Dolphin

Tesla do not advertise but have provided the lion's share of battery electric cars, a total of over 7 million at the time of writing. At the bottom end (although more expensive than most other makes of battery electric cars), there is the Model 3. This provides great value for money compared to the other previous models of Tesla cars (and other makes of battery electric car) as it has similar range to the more expensive older Tesla models and the same level of automation. It is about the same size as a BMW 3 series and is a conventional saloon, not a hatchback.

The Tesla Model Y is a SUV (Sports Utility Vehicle) style car of similar size to the Model 3. It is often considered the best family EV car in reviews.

Tesla Model 3 Highland

Tesla Model Y

Polestar is another battery electric car. Polestar 2 is their entry level car. Polestar 4 is a compact SUV and Polestar 3 is a full SUV.

Polestar 2

Volkswagen have a number of offerings including the ID.5:

VW ID.5

If you want an even larger battery electric car, a US style pickup, try the Tesla Cybertruck (not available in the UK or Europe), the GMC Hummer and the Rivian R1T.

Some newer cars allow you to make use of the battery for non-car use. V2L (Vehicle to Line) produces mains electricity, for use with a kettle for example when camping by plugging a special cable into the charging port. (See *"Getting Further Information"* chapter). Another way you can use the car battery is with V2G (Vehicle to Grid). You can store energy from your home solar cells during the day and get your car battery to power your house at night (Make sure you have enough battery charge next day for travel!). Check to see if your new car has these features. Not all do. (See *"Getting Further Information"* chapter for information on V2G).

The disadvantage of buying or leasing a new car compared to a used car is depreciation. Furthermore, at present most new battery electric cars are more expensive than equivalent petrol or diesel cars although in 2025, some EV cars are approaching petrol or diesel car prices.

There are a couple of MG cars worthy of mention:

MG4 EV
The MG4 EV is an SUV and this "Lamborghini orange" version could easily be mistaken for a Lamborghini Urus SUV which costs more than 10 times the cost of an MG4. So, if you want an expensive looking car why not go for the MG4 EV.

MG Cyberster
The MG Cyberster is an open top sports car with an electric roof and scissor doors!

9 BUYING A USED CAR

Just because you are buying a used car, there is no need to buy a wreck. Although battery electric cars, in modern form are still relatively new, enough years have passed since their introduction for used car sales to be well established now.

Buying your used car from a dealer will usually cost you more than a private purchase, but in return you get a warranty and dealer attention. There are dealers who sell a variety of different makes of car including petrol and diesel cars. There are also specialists who sell used battery electric cars (with expertise in a single make or a variety of makes).

Finally, it is possible to strike a bargain by buying privately. In this last category you need to be aware of the Latin saying "Caveat Emptor". This translates to "Be careful what you buy, there is no going back" - those Romans were very succinct.

Battery electric cars depreciate, like any other car, so one advantage of buying a used battery electric car is that the price is lower than a new one.

Historically the reason for the large depreciation of most used battery electric cars is that there has been only a small demand for second hand battery electric cars as potential buyers have been nervous about how long the battery will last. The life of the battery is covered in more detail in the "*Lifetime Considerations*" chapter. Suffice to say that battery life has proved to be far longer than most people would expect. Batteries can fail in rare cases and they can prematurely age - in Arizona there have been a few problems with older battery technologies. However most batteries gracefully degrade - their range reduces by a small amount each year. It is usually a matter for the owner to decide when it needs replacing. Do use your car. If you do not, the battery will still degrade with time.

Battery electric cars have been available since 2009, so there should be used battery electric cars available for every budget. Older cars have a range which will be less than when new and you should be aware that older cars, even when they were new, had a shorter range than new cars available now.

A 2011 onwards Nissan Leaf can be found at reasonable cost. There are a number of alternatives if you can afford more. For example, the i3 is more expensive but still much less than the price of a new one.

BMW i3

The Renault Zoë has been a popular small hatchback car for some time

Renault Zoë

An even more expensive but long range luxury car option can be found in a Tesla. If you are buying a used Tesla Model S or Model X there are other benefits - An older Tesla can make use of free charging from the Tesla network of chargers for travelling long distances, whereas owners of new Teslas need to pay for use of the chargers.

The Model S is a luxury, very large hatchback. The Tesla Model X is a very large SUV. This can be configured to fit seven adults comfortably. Model 3s and Model Ys are available now too.

Tesla Model S   **Tesla Model X**

It is important to try to find out what it is like to live with a car of the type you are planning to purchase. If you are buying from a dealer, you may be able to try it for a while, in which case the information in the previous chapter about trialing a new car applies. However, if you are planning to buy privately, this is unlikely to be possible. I would suggest that in this case you try to rent one for at least a day or two to find out what it is like. See "*Getting Further Information*" chapter. Failing this try to find out what the experience of other drivers is by looking at owner group forums. Most makes have one. Again, see "*Getting Further Information*" chapter.

Buying a used Tesla gives you full access to the best fast charging (supercharger) network that is available for charging on a journey.

Before buying a used battery electric car it pays to try to establish how well the car has been treated. A good service history, recording regular servicing carried out in accordance with the manufacturer 's recommendations is always a help.

It is useful (but unfortunately normally very difficult) to find out the following:
1. Is the car frequently charged to 100%? (Usually not good)
2. Is it charged often either at home or work (or both) rather than being charged regularly at the higher rate obtainable from high speed chargers? (A good thing),
3. Is it often driven until the battery is flat /close to 0% (Not good),
4. Is it often left in a state of low charge? (Not good),
5. Is it frequently charged when nearly full? (Not usually good),
6. Is it left fully charged and not used for a while? (Not good)
7. Does it have a high mileage (more than 25,000 miles a year)? (Not usually good),
8. Does it have a low mileage (less than 4000 miles a year)? (Not usually good).

All of these factors affect the battery quality. Some cars such as the Nissan Leaf, have a means of indicating the quality of the battery (this is not the state of charge or percentage charged). On the Nissan Leaf dashboard, where it indicates state of charge (percent charged) and current range in miles, around the outside is a number of illuminated graduations. There are 12 when new and, in the photo, below, a 3-year-old 50,000 mile example is shown to have 11. The battery has degraded to the point where it has lost one graduation. With that mileage and age that is a reasonable degradation and does not affect the range very much but if the same car had, say, only 8 or 9, it would indicate a harshly treated car.

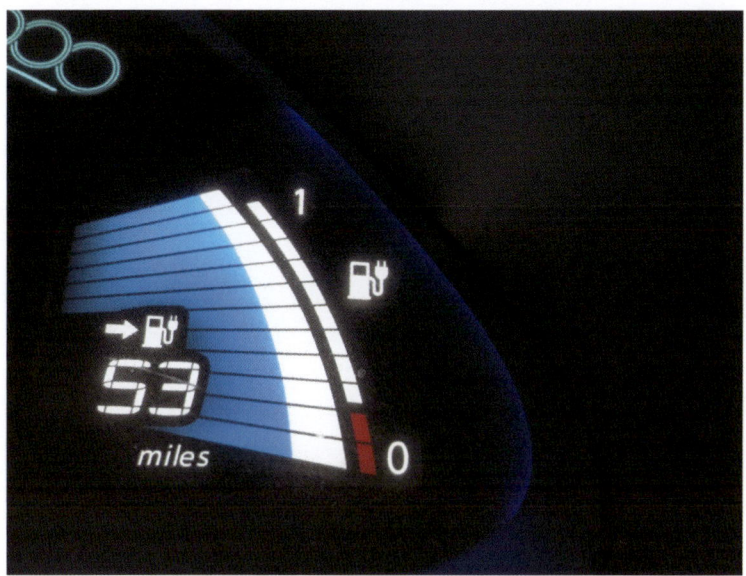

Nissan Leaf with a battery state of 11 out of 12 graduations

Some service records will indicate how good the battery was at the last service. If not, it might be worth phoning the place where it was last serviced to find out if more information on the battery status is available.

The photo above demonstrates another point. The range for a full battery is shown as 53 miles. This photo was taken at winter when most recent journeys had been short. In summer with recent long journeys, for the same car this would go up to 86 miles.

Lastly, one disadvantage of buying a used car is that the technology is changing fast and one factor which is changing in particular is the energy storage which is linked strongly to the range available. For example, a top of the range Tesla bought new a few years ago, might have 75% of the energy storage capability of one bought now and a new one will charge much faster from a supercharger.

10 CHARGING AT HOME

There is no need to bring the car inside your house to charge it. Indeed, it is wise not to do so for all sorts of reasons, not least tyre marks on the carpets. Nevertheless, home charging is remarkably easy to carry out in most circumstances. In many ways it is easier than charging a mobile phone. For one thing, the cable connectors are bigger and easier to fit into the sockets.

Firstly, let's begin with those who are fortunate enough to have off road parking. Typically, charging at home is carried out overnight, so that the car has maybe a full charge but certainly a higher charge the next day. It obviates the need to fill up at a garage and even if your mileage means you need to charge every night, this is still less bother than filling up a petrol or diesel car.

A typical charging scenario is as follows - A button is pressed or a lever pulled in the car to open a flap revealing a connector. This may be at the front, at the side, or at the back of the car, depending on the car manufacturer. The charging lead from an installed charger is then simply plugged into the connector on the car. Charging then happens automatically. The following diagrams show how this happens for a Tesla. There are a few variations to this procedure which can be identified in the manual for your particular car.

Press button to open flap   **Connector open**

Plug in charging lead

Unplugging is even more straightforward but you need to check the manual for your car to find out the steps to unplug the car.

Some cars or apps for the car allow you to specify times to charge, levels to charge to (for example to 80% of a full battery, rather than to 100%) and times to heat or cool the car. The latter is very useful to prepare the car for safety and comfort before you get into it. It may also help with the range by ensuring the battery is at a suitable temperature for highest efficiency. If you heat or cool the car while it is plugged in for charging then you will get a much better range than if you set off and heat or cool the car after you have set off. Setting different charge levels, for example to 80% rather than 100% is for extending the life of your battery. This is covered in detail in the *"Lifetime Considerations"* chapter. Typically, an 80% charge would be used for short journeys or occasional use while 100% would be used only for longer journeys. Some cars allow you to choose the end time for the charging. If you use this facility to coincide with the time when you need to drive the car, it will warm the battery, making the car ready for efficient use. The instruction manual for your car will show you if any of these facilities are available and how to use them.

To charge your car at home, you need three elements - the car, a charger and somewhere where the charging lead can be run from the charger to the car. If you have a drive or a garage this is straightforward.

The most robust means of charging at home is to use an installed charge point, usually wall mounted. You need a qualified electrical fitter to fit one of these and depending on the power rating, you may need modifications to your domestic supply which a fitter can advise about.

You can mount your home charger on an outside wall or, if you have a garage, on the inside wall of the garage.

An example of a wall-mounted charger is shown in the photograph below.

An installed charger

I prefer to have a "tethered" charging lead. This means the charging lead is permanently attached (tethered) to the charger and therefore always available for use. Some people prefer an "untethered" charger. This has a socket on the charger in the above diagram and a separate charging lead which is either kept in the house or in the car which needs to be brought out and connected for each charging session. An untethered lead will allow for different plugs that fit in the car so if you have two cars with different plugs this might be a better option than a tethered lead.

One of the main things you will have to decide is what power you want for your charger. The more powerful the charger, the shorter the charging time. People often choose a higher power charger than they really need. The standard ratings are 3.7kW, 7kW, 11kW and 22kW. The most popular at present are 3.7kW and 7kW.

You will need to check how quickly your car will charge at each of these power levels and judge for yourself if this will be adequate. It does depend on how big your battery is and how long you will be at home, not needing to use the car. For example, I use a 7kW charger for my Tesla. You should not need to alter your house wiring significantly for a 3.7kW or 7kW charger but if you really feel you need an 11kW or 22kW charger, you will need a 3 phase supply. You also need to check if your car can make use of the power if you go for a higher powered charger. Your fitter will be able to advise you.

You can now get cordless chargers whereby equipment is installed under your drive or under the floor of your garage and you simply park the car over it. The advantage of these is that they do not need connecting as above and are not visible.

A very simple form of "untethered" charger is a portable charger. It is a unit with a charging lead and connector which is portable and can be carried in your car. It is typically supplied with the car. This may be connected to an external domestic socket. This arrangement is mainly intended for emergencies where there are no nearby public charge points and you are away from home. Be careful about using it on a more regular basis as conventional mains sockets can easily burn out if used for this purpose. A more robust arrangement which is less prone to burn out is a special socket called a commando socket as shown below. You also need to be careful about protection from water ingress when it is raining, although they are usually resistant to water to an extent. People who prefer not to install a permanent charger charge their cars at home using this arrangement.

Portable charger   **Commando socket**
using domestic socket

If you do not have off road parking, as many do not, there are other options. If there is space on your road outside your house, this is a clever idea from Kerbocharge (See *"Getting Further Information"* chapter for details).

Kerbocharge installation

If you live in a flat you may be fortunate enough to have a designated car parking space.

Dedicated charging car park space at flats

You can get a grant for a charger for a flat if it is practical. There are a few ingenious solutions including running a cable out of a window *(See "Getting Further Information" chapter)*. If home charging is not practical then it will be necessary either to use public charge points or (if applicable) to charge at work. Public charge points are illustrated and covered in the next chapter *"Travelling Long Distances"*. Alternately, some enterprising Local Authorities are providing chargers in lamp posts. *(See "Getting Further Information" chapter).*

These chargers make use of the lower power demand that has arisen from using LED street lights. If you have to park on the road at your home this could be helpful.

'blink' lamp post charging point

To all intents and purposes, charging at work is similar to charging at home. Indeed, the chargers are the same as those available for charging at home. The difference being that it is done during your working hours and the car will have increased its charge by the time you are ready to go home.

There are Government grants available for chargers at work if you want to convince your employer to fit one or more chargers. See "*Getting Further Information*" chapter for details of how to find these.

Failing any of these options, you will need to charge at public charge points. See "*Driving Long Distances*" chapter for details on using public charge points.

11 DRIVING LONG DISTANCES

Your journey may normally be such that you can drive 'there and back' without charging, or charge at your destination, for example when staying at a hotel which has something similar to a home charger.

However, if you do want to travel beyond the range of your car, you will have to charge part of the way along your journey in much the same way as you would need to refuel in a petrol or diesel car if your fuel was insufficient to get you to your destination and back.

In the UK there are a number of high speed charge points, often at motorway service stations suitable for charging reasonably quickly. Typically, a substantial recharge, (up to 80% of the battery capacity) might take 30 minutes or less which is a good time to buy a coffee, have a nap or refresh yourself. The oldest type of high speed charger is a CHAdeMO type. This is a technical term which comes from the Japanese meaning "Have a cup of tea" - charge speeds have now increased to the point where you may not have enough time to have a cup of tea. The CHAdeMO refers to the type of charging plug for high speed charging. The more recent common standard which applies to virtually every new car is the Combined Charging System (CCS).

The planning you can do is to check what charge points are available on your route and whether they are working or not. There are a number of apps available for a mobile phone. Zap map is one I use. See the "*Getting Further Information*" chapter for suitable phone or computer apps for planning. Equally your sat nav may be able to let you plan your route and tell you where you can charge en route. The Tesla sat nav tells you as you travel how many bays are in use and how many are free at Tesla Super Charging sites. Most new cars now have a built-in app with charge point locations.

When my son and I drove from Land's End to John o'Groats and back, gaining a Guinness World Record for charging time, we did the bare minimum of planning. In fact, when we got to John o'Groats we found a high speed charger we did not know existed. I am sure that most people who drive in a petrol or diesel car do not check what garages are available en route to fill up. The network of charging stations is so good these days it is not absolutely necessary to plan with a battery electric car. However, if you do not check availability, it is advisable to charge when you can in case the next charging site is faulty.

Although the charging network is well developed, the means to pay is not. Some chargers require you to use a phone app, which it is preferable to set up before you leave. Many allow a credit or debit card to be used at the charger. At the time of writing there is a substantial network of fast charge points in England, Wales and Northern Ireland operated by Gridserve and their phone app will get you access to any of their charge points. In Scotland, ChargePlace Scotland operate a large number of charge points and give access to some in the north of England too. ChargePlace Scotland operate through their charge card, which you can apply for, or a phone app which you need to register. There are other suppliers too. See the "*Getting Further Information*" chapter for further details.

It is worth researching charging accounts to get the right one for you. Some charge a monthly fee and are particularly useful for people who frequently charge their car on a journey. Others charge more per charge but with no monthly fee. I tend to have accounts which do not have a monthly fee. In fact, the charge points I use most frequently en route (apart from Tesla superchargers which are free for my Tesla) are Gridserve ones.

When you need to use a high speed charger, you need to find it first. You may find your sat nav can do this for you and may suggest when you need to charge. If not, there are phone apps such as Zap Map, which can tell you where there are nearby charge points. See the "*Getting Further Information*" chapter for details of Zap Map and other similar apps.

Having found the charge point, you need to park your car so that the charger is close to where you plug in a charger cable on your car. Each high speed charger has its own cable so you don't have to be very close and importantly you will not need your own cable.

Motorway Service Gridserve Chargers

Taking the Gridserve chargers as an example, get out of the car and approach the charger. Approach the screen on the charger and follow the instructions to connect your car and pay.

You will finish charging, either because the app has timed you out (a typical time might be 45 minutes) or because you select stop charging on the app or charger screen. You then need to disconnect the cable and you can drive away with the car charged and hopefully the driver refreshed. Note it is really bad form to park at a charger if you are not charging.

Tesla Super Chargers are even easier to use with a Tesla. Simply connect the cable by plugging into the socket you use for charging at home. When you have finished, press stop charging on the screen in the car.

The Supercharger below was the most northerly in the world, several hundred miles inside the Arctic Circle. If you have a Tesla and visit a part of the world where there are few superchargers, you may find it useful to get a CCS adaptor from your friendly Tesla store if you have an older Tesla like mine so you can use it at public charge points. Newer Teslas will operate on non-Tesla chargers without the need for an adaptor.

Tesla Super Charger

If you do have a problem with a high speed charger, telephone the number on the charger. If you find yourself some distance from a high speed charger, for example due to a faulty site, do not panic. Look for an alternative, possibly a lower power charger, if necessary, using an app such as Zap Map. Drive slowly and you will conserve range. It is highly unlikely you will not find somewhere to charge but if you do run out, you will have to call a recovery service such as the AA.

12 DRIVING ABROAD

Driving abroad is similar to driving long distances in the UK. The big difference is you will need apps to operate the public chargers, which are typically different from the apps you use in the UK. (See *"Getting Further Information"* chapter). Otherwise, the instructions in the chapter "*Driving Long Distances*" chapter apply.

I recently drove to Iceland (via a ferry from Denmark) and needed to use an Icelandic charger. I was able to download the app from the app store while I was standing next to the charger so do not feel you always have to do a lot before you travel to use charge points abroad.

However, when you arrive at your destination you may want to charge from a domestic socket using your portable UK charger which typically is supplied with the car. (See *"Home Charging"* chapter). If this is the case you will need to use an adaptor to fit the non-UK mains socket. Make sure that the adaptor is robust enough to do the job and the domestic socket is modern as otherwise you may find you plunge the place you are staying at into darkness. A typical adaptor such as one you can buy at an airport is rarely adequate. The *"Getting Further Information"* chapter shows how you can obtain more robust adaptors such as the one below, which has a European style plug at one end and a UK domestic style socket at the other end.

European plug to UK socket adaptor

If you own a Tesla, life is much simpler; you just use Superchargers as you would in the UK and if necessary, Tesla destination chargers. Incidentally. there are Tesla Superchargers in Iceland as well was the whole of Europe.

Irrespective of whether you are travelling in a battery electric car, certain regulations apply which do not in the UK. For example, if you wear glasses or contact lenses, when driving in Spain you need to have a spare pair of glasses, kept in easy reach of the driver 's seat. (See *"Getting Further Information"* chapter).

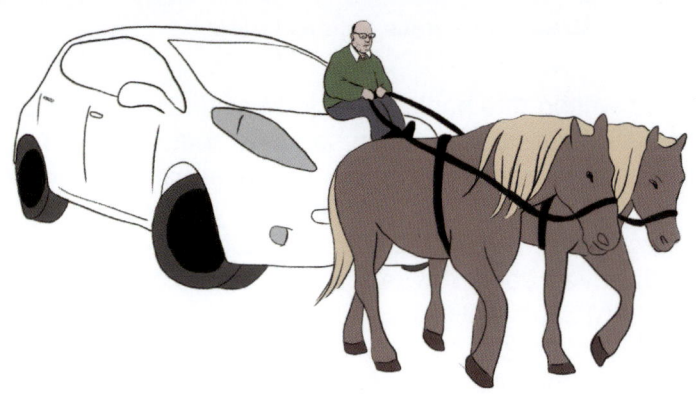

13 HYBRID CARS

A hybrid car has two forms of power. A hybrid car normally has a conventional petrol (or diesel) internal combustion engine and also the components for a battery electric car - a battery and a motor/generator. This allows operation either from the battery like a battery electric car or by means of the petrol (or diesel) engine. They offer long range from the petrol or diesel engine but use the battery and motor/generator to reduce the amount of time the petrol or diesel engine is needed, leading to quiet emission free driving when the car is electrically rather than petrol or diesel engine driven and an overall decreased fuel consumption compared to a conventional car with just a petrol/diesel engine. The additional components in a hybrid make it more expensive and heavier than a conventional petrol or diesel car. It may be more unreliable due to the additional complexity too. Furthermore, the battery tends to be smaller than a battery electric car and can come under more stress leading to a shorter life.

The battery of a hybrid is typically charged when the car is braked, but also by the petrol or diesel engine when the petrol or diesel engine is being used to drive the car. Most recently built hybrid cars allow you to charge the battery from chargers at home, at work or at public charge points. This ensures you have a charged battery before you set off and it is then not essential to drive the car from the engine and does increase the opportunity to drive the car under electric power.

When I first started writing this book, I was in two minds as to whether to include a chapter on hybrid cars. I can see they could be more likely to be attractive to current drivers of petrol or diesel cars than battery electric cars, not least because you are not wholly dependent on the battery being charged to travel long distances. Indeed, you could drive a hybrid car without even being aware that it has an electric capability as most hybrid cars will automatically switch between electric or petrol/diesel. They may be a good route towards reducing dependency on fossil fuels for those people who are reluctant to make the full switch to battery electric.

There are several different categories of hybrid cars ranging from micro to full hybrid. A micro hybrid car will simply switch off the engine if you are stationary at traffic lights and switch the engine on when you want to move off. There is no capability to drive with the electric motor alone but it does decrease fuel consumption and reduces emissions when in stationary traffic. A large number of modern cars have this facility and most drivers of such cars are not even aware that they are driving a micro hybrid car. This is often referred to as stop-start technology. At the other end of the spectrum, a full hybrid car is capable of being driven by the electric motor alone, typically when setting off, reversing and in town for short journeys. Providing the battery has been charged sufficiently, full hybrid cars will start off on the electric motor and automatically switch to petrol or diesel when the battery is no longer sufficiently charged. Some early hybrids did not have a facility to charge the battery at chargers. The more recently built hybrids have this facility and are known as "plug-in" hybrids. Some manufacturers have controversially used the lack of a plug in facility as a selling point! They have been branded as "self-charging hybrids".

The plug-in hybrid car shown below has an impressive claimed range of 78 miles on battery. It is made in China by BYD who make the largest number of battery electric cars in the world.

BYD Seal Plugin Hybrid

The following is a list of other manufacturers of popular full hybrid cars:

Volvo, Audi, Kia, Hyundai, Honda, Infiniti, Toyota, Skoda, Ford, Vauxhall, BMW, VW, Lexus, Mitsubishi, Mercedes, Renault.

There are many other manufacturers. More exotic examples include Ferrari and Porsche.

To conclude - A hybrid, even a micro hybrid, reduces emissions and reduces fuel consumption when compared to a conventional petrol or diesel car. A hybrid is typically more expensive and heavier than a conventional petrol or diesel car as well as being more complicated. A hybrid is not dependent on its battery being charged for long journeys so it has that advantage over battery electric cars. However, a battery electric car has no exhaust emissions which a hybrid car does have when the petrol or diesel engine is being used and a battery electric car places less stress on its battery.

14 HYDROGEN FUEL CELL CARS

A car which runs on water? Not quite. Few people realise that the Apollo moon missions could not have taken place without hydrogen providing the electricity needed in the space capsules to support the human crew. Battery technology at the time was too bulky and heavy. Instead, a hydrogen fuel cell was used to produce electricity from hydrogen and oxygen carried onboard. The subsequent space shuttles also used hydrogen.

The same technology can be used in a car. Refuelling is actually quicker than recharging a battery. It takes about the same time as a petrol or diesel car to refuel. Like battery cars, there are no toxic emissions (only water vapour) and the range can be better than battery cars. This looks like the ideal alternative to a petrol or diesel car and yet, Elon Musk, who amongst other things has been behind the popular mass-produced battery electric cars (TESLA) has publicly referred to hydrogen fuel cells as fool cells. We are not all driving hydrogen cars so what is preventing us from doing so? Let's start by looking at the positive practicalities before examining the drawbacks.

A Toyota Mirai hydrogen car

As can be seen above, a hydrogen car looks much like a petrol car. This one seats five people with plenty of space in the boot. It can be filled up at a hydrogen refuelling station as below

A Shell hydrogen refuelling station

The nozzle and hose on the left-hand side of what looks like a large petrol pump deliver compressed hydrogen gas at a high pressure to the car. The hydrogen is produced on site from water and (preferably) sustainable electricity

The photo below, shows the receptacle for the hydrogen tank on a hydrogen car which is very similar to a petrol car. Refuelling will be familiar to anyone who has filled a diesel or petrol car.

Filler cover closed   **Filler cover open**

Cap over receptacle removed

So why are there over a million battery electric cars in the UK since they started to become popular in 2009 and only 300 hydrogen cars even though billions of euros have been spent on developing hydrogen cars over the last 20 years?

The answers are as follows:

1) Lack of refuelling infrastructure - actually there are some Shell garages with such infrastructure at some strategic locations in the UK but at least one has closed due to lack of demand.

2) Cost - the cost is similar to a Tesla Model S but the two main manufacturers - Toyota and Hyundai tend to lease their cars, partly to ensure that safety critical maintenance is carried out.

3) Perceived safety issues - there is a great video on YouTube (See *"Getting Further Information"* chapter) where a hydrogen car and a petrol car are both set alight and left to burn out. There is nothing but the burnt metal body left of the petrol car but the hydrogen car looks in showroom condition. Hydrogen is lighter than air and the flames flow into the sky away from the car. However, maintenance is more important than for any other type of car.

4) Efficiency - a fuel cell is only 50% efficient and there is further loss in producing hydrogen. If the hydrogen is produced locally from sustainable sources, this is less of an issue.

5) Public enthusiasm - battery electric cars have attracted a large number of enthusiasts. Hydrogen cars have not. So much so that the hydrogen refuelling station at Cobham motorway services on the M25 has been closed due to insufficient use.

6) Battery electric cars can be charged at home at a fraction of the cost of the equivalent hydrogen or petrol (the cost of hydrogen is similar to petrol at service stations)

A battery electric car can be built, seating 5 or more adults, with a 400-mile range and with a good performance, but the resources, volume and weight needed for battery electric trucks, battery electric trains and battery electric marine applications together with limited need for infrastructure makes hydrogen alternatives for these much more attractive even with the lower efficiency. I have finished working with Porterbrook and the University of Birmingham on the UK 's first and second hydrogen trains. I am now working on the UK's first hydrogen shunting locomotive.

15 ELECTRIC BIKES

An electric bike (or e-bike) is similar to a conventional bicycle but with a battery and motor to augment the effort you provide on the pedals. If it is many years since you have ridden a bicycle, you may be wary, but please read on. Electric bikes allow you to get some exercise as you would on a conventional bicycle but they make it easier by allowing you to choose how much support you get from the battery and motor. In any case, even if you choose the minimum support, you will find going uphill is virtually effortless. This means that you can easily double the distance you would feel comfortable cycling. For most people that would mean that in theory you could get rid of your car!

Electric bikes are easy to use - modern ones simply add to your effort automatically as the control system recognises the speed at which you are turning the pedals and applies additional energy to help you accordingly. Typically, there are different settings you can apply, depending on how much help you want. I often select the minimum (eco) setting which on my bicycle provides up to the same amount of energy as I apply to the pedals when I want a lot of exercise. Otherwise, I use an intermediate setting (tour), but I could select the highest (turbo) setting and find that I get three times more electric energy than I apply to the pedals. On this setting, you would not even realise you were going up a hill. Electric bikes are considerably better for the environment than cars, buses or trains. For example, my electric bike shown below has a battery range considerably better than my old Nissan Leaf car but has a battery size one thirtieth of the car.

One of the author's e-bikes

If you have not ridden an electric bike before, do try one. Most bicycle shops will let you try one for no payment. If you are thinking of buying one, my recommendation would be for one with a motor near the pedals rather than in either the front or back wheel. This is because you gain the benefit of the gears on your e-bike. My e-bike even has an indicator to tell you when to change gear to make it easy to pedal at all times. I recommend you try a few to see which one suits you. One point to note is that, by law, the electric assistance is stopped above 15.5 mph. As an electric bike is typically heavier than a conventional bike, you will find you have to pedal harder than you would on a conventional bike, above this speed. I used to use a conventional bicycle regularly but since I have bought an electric bicycle, I have not gone back. I also have a folding e-bike which I find very convenient I confess I use my e-bike more than either of my electric cars.

The author's folding e-bike

16 BATTERY ELECTRIC AND HYBRID VANS

Battery electric vans are widely used for what is known as last mile deliveries. They have a number of advantages over diesel or petrol vans for this application. They are quiet, emission free, low cost to run and increasingly important, are not subject to emission taxes in cities.

The Nissan eV200 was one of the first to arrive on the scene but since then offerings including from Citroën, Fiat, Ford, Peugeot, Renault, Mercedes, Vauxhall and Volkswagen have appeared.

Clockwise from top Mercedes, VW, Nissan, Ford

There are therefore a number of different manufacturers of vans to choose from. Some used vans are now available for purchase as well as new ones.

The Ford Transit as an example, can allow you to use the van battery to power tools rather than using a petrol generator or very long extension leads.

Notice the snow on the windscreen of the Nissan van above. Cold temperatures are not a significant problem for vans (or cars) although range is reduced in colder temperatures so it is best to make sure your range will be sufficient in the coldest temperature you are likely to encounter.

For longer range an alternative is a hybrid van and as with cars these might be a good way to get into electric drives.

A Diesel Electric Hybrid Ford Transit Van

Finally, it will please many readers that the classic VW camper van is also available in electric form. There are other makes of camper vans but this is the one which is most popularly associated with camper vans

VW ID. Buzz

These chapters apply equally to vans as to cars:

The Pros and Cons of Battery Electric Cars, Economics, Lifetime Considerations, Are You Saving the Planet? Buying or Leasing a New Car, buying a Used Car, Charging at Home, Driving Long Distances, Driving Abroad and Hybrid Cars.

The best advice I can give you, if you are considering leasing or buying a new or used van, is to try it, preferably in winter, when range tends to be at its lowest.

www.jeffvehicles.com

17 BATTERY ELECTRIC AND HYDROGEN FUEL CELL TRUCKS

There are two main options to replace a diesel engined truck with an electric alternative. The first is battery electric and the second is hydrogen fuel cell. There is interest in other alternatives including biofuel and use of hydrogen in internal combustion engines but these are not electric alternatives, although they are the lowest capital cost alternatives. ULEMCo for example, offer hydrogen dual fuel options. (See *"Getting Further Information"* chapter).

ULEMCo Dual Fuel Hydrogen /Diesel Tractor

At present, most interest seems to be in electric trucks, either battery electric or hydrogen fuel cell.

A hydrogen fuel cell, electric motor and controller are about the same weight as an equivalent diesel engine but the fuel storage - gas tanks are light. They are made from aluminium and carbon fibre. Batteries are heavy so it is likely that for long range as required by tractor units, a fuel cell tractor can be made lighter than an equivalent battery tractor. A tractor needs to meet a minimum weight for traction purposes so the weight difference of the equipment may not be a significant issue.

ULEMCo make hydrogen fuel cell trucks. More about ULEMCo can be found in the *"Getting Further Information"* chapter.

ULEMCo Hydrogen Fuel Cell Powered Ambulance

The ULEMCo Fuel Cell ambulance above is a good application, from a refuelling point of view, because ambulances can be refuelled from designated locations.

It is important truck operators consider fuel infrastructure. It is interesting to note that much of the hydrogen refuelling infrastructure has followed early interest in hydrogen buses and therefore tends to be in cities. This interest has not been followed up more recently because many bus operators are now investing in battery electric rather than hydrogen powered buses. At least one refuelling station in the UK has been closed due to insufficient use. See "*Getting Further Information*" chapter for details of how to find current UK hydrogen refuelling stations.

For shorter range trucks, where a limited size battery is sufficient, battery electric trucks make sense but there are a number of longer range battery electric trucks emerging.

MAN make an eTGX battery electric tractor. MAN, also make rigid trucks such as the eTGL and eTGS. MAN trucks typically have a range of more than 400km. They are smoother and quieter than their diesel equivalents. They have one pedal operation and aerodynamic cameras instead of mirrors.

Volvo also have a battery electric tractor. It is based on their diesel tractor and is called the Volvo Aero FH Electric. It, too, has aerodynamic cameras instead of mirrors.

Volvo Aero FH Electric tractor

At present battery vehicle charging has been mainly for cars and vans. There are extensive networks of these. If considering a battery electric truck, it is important to know where you can charge and if you can use chargers designed for electric cars, typically Combined Charging System (CCS). Existing truck high speed public recharging points include Rivington services between Preston and Manchester on the M61, and Dundee also Aberdeen, where the coach operator Ember has opened their sites for HGVs. Many others are planned to be open soon.

There is a new standard being developed for trucks. This is the Megawatt Charging System (MCS) which allows much high powers for charging and therefore shorter charging times. The charging plug is much larger than the one used for CCS.

These chapters may also be of interest to truck operators:
The Pros and Cons of Battery Electric Cars, Economics, Lifetime Considerations, Are You Saving the Planet?, Buying or Leasing a New Car, buying a Used Car, Charging at Home, Driving Long Distances, Driving Abroad, Hybrid Cars, Hydrogen Fuel Cell Cars and Battery

Electric and *Hybrid Vans.*

18 CONVERTING PETROL CARS

At present, car manufacturers struggle to make a profit on new electric cars even with the economies of scale. It is therefore not surprising that converting a petrol car to battery electric is costly. Petrol or diesel engines and gearboxes are relatively cheap, compared to the equipment needed to run a battery electric car. There are a number of companies that will convert your car to battery electric but it usually only makes sense for special cars such as classic or vintage cars due to the expense (See *"Getting Further information"* chapter). The author is currently converting his 1953 Morris Minor to battery electric as an interesting exercise and to ensure all his vehicles are battery electric.

There are a number of components needed as a minimum for conversion:
• An electric motor,
• A battery and battery management system,
• An inverter to convert the battery DC to AC suitable for the motor,
• Contactors to switch and isolate the large DC currents,
• Cables,
• Fuses and
• Isolating switches.

There are only a few suppliers in the UK for these components. (See *"Getting Further Information"* chapter).

The electric motor should be matched to the performance required. I chose a smaller motor to closely match the existing Morris Minor engine performance.

Electric Motor for Morris Minor

In the above photo, a new plate has been provided to connect the motor to the gearbox and a new clutch has been fitted. It is often not necessary to retain the original gearbox and clutch but the author wants the car to look original from inside the car and outside.

There are a number of books on car conversion but to do it yourself requires a depth of knowledge on the subject. In addition, you will need to get your converted car inspected. (See *"Getting Further Information"* chapter).

19 HISTORY

Most people will be astonished to read that battery electric cars were invented before petrol cars and well before diesel cars. First prototypes of electric cars appeared in the 1830s. The invention of the lead acid battery in 1859 with further improvements to battery technology enabled more practical examples. An early UK electric car was built, in 1880, by inventor Magnus Volk and is illustrated below.

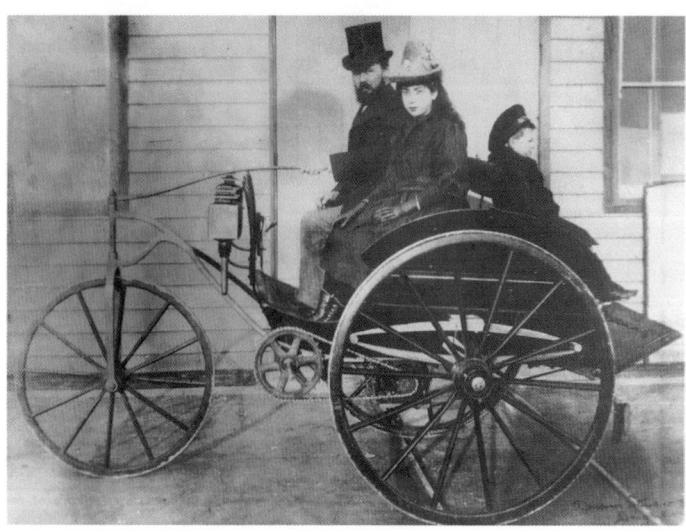

Magnus Volk in his electric dog cart

Magnus Volk is pictured outside his railway offices. He was the inventor of the first electric railway in the world. It actually ran on tracks near the sea at Brighton. His electric railway is still in use today and runs along the sea front. Recently, another of his inventions has been restored - a gilded copper sphere on the clock tower in the centre of Brighton which rises and falls every hour. (See *"Getting Further Information"* chapter).

The first golden age for battery electric cars was between the 1890s and the early 1910s. The world land speed record was held by battery electric cars until 1902 when the 65.8 mile an hour record was broken by a steam car. Electric taxis were on the streets of London during this time. Battery electric cars were popular as they were more attractive than petrol or steam cars. They were easy and quick to start, clean, and easy to drive. The main problem was range although they proved popular for city use.

Battery electric cars declined by the 1920s when mass production made petrol cars cheaper. At the same time petrol cars began to be fitted with electric starter motors, overcoming another obstacle in their use. Development of good roads allowed more comfortable long distance travelling and increased the need for more range than electric cars could offer at that time.

Battery electric vehicles continued in niche areas, the ubiquitous milk float being a good example. Milk was delivered early in the morning and the frequent stop-start and necessity to be quiet to avoid waking customers combined with a requirement for only a short range made the technology highly suitable. Large numbers of lead acid batteries were used.

Interest in battery electric cars was revived in the early 1970s due to the energy crisis. The 1972 Leyland Crompton prototype shown below was typical of the period.

1972 Leyland Crompton prototype

These were heavy and impractical, relying on lead acid batteries. The Leyland Crompton used Mini parts but despite being small, it was one third heavier than a Mini. It had a top speed of 33 mph and a range of only 40 miles. Mass production of these types of cars never happened.

Under pressure from the state of California in the USA, a number of battery electric cars were produced by mainstream car manufacturers, such as Ford, General Motors and Honda in the 1990s. The cars were typically leased and were highly popular with the people using them but the manufacturers appeared to have another agenda exemplified in the documentary film "Who killed the Electric Car?" (See *"Getting Further Information"* chapter). GM, much to the disgust of a number of people using their EV1 cars, repossessed the cars at the end of the lease period, refusing to sell them and subsequently destroyed most of them.

The real breakthrough for battery electric cars came through the development of the lithium-ion battery. In the early 2000s, a number of short range but normal speed battery electric cars were developed culminating in the launch of the Mitsubishi I-MiEV in

2009, a battery electric car owned by the author and, a year later, the Nissan Leaf, also owned by the author.

Perhaps the most remarkable car of the time was the Tesla Roadster which was first sold in 2008. This had an amazing range and performance compared to all other battery electric cars. The sales of the Roadster funded the Tesla Model S which again was a game changer as it is a large 5-seater capable of being driven hundreds of miles at 70mph. This was launched in 2012. It is the author's favourite car! Sales of the Model S and subsequently the Model X, funded the smaller and cheaper Model 3 and subsequently the Model Y.

Hybrid cars have a long history too. Dr. Ferdinand Porsche built the first car to combine an internal combustion engine with electric motors, albeit without a battery. There was some interest in hybrid vehicles after this time.

The photo below shows the 1927 Lanchester hybrid which did include a battery. By the 1930s all interest in hybrids had disappeared until 2000 when Toyota introduced their Prius, so we are now celebrating two and a half decades of modern hybrid cars.

1927 Lanchester hybrid

20 FUTURE TRENDS

The general trend with batteries and charging infrastructure is for range to increase, cost of batteries to fall and charging time to decrease. All of these factors are likely to accelerate the switch to battery electric cars because perceived barriers to use are being broken down.

Other technologies, such as super capacitors are being developed with even shorter charging times, however at present the problem is cost and weight. (See *"Getting Further Information"* chapter)

There is an interesting trend in the UK, particularly in cities for a smaller number of young people to learn to drive. There are several reasons for this - improved public transport, lower cost of taxis and higher cost of car ownership, especially insurance; also, a greater concern for the environment.

A typical car, whether battery electric or not, is used for a small proportion of a day and therefore it is not cost efficient. Improving automation leading towards fully autonomous driving is likely to result in less of a need for full ownership and more car sharing. In London, recent technology has made it relatively easy to rent a car without the need to book in advance and without the need for the user to deal with human sales staff. Typically, the car can be collected from one place, used and then left at a different location. (See *"Getting Further Information"* chapter)

A potential use for battery electric cars when they are not being driven is to stabilise electricity supplies. Solar cells which are increasingly being installed on household roofs generate during daylight hours when electricity is not at a high demand. At peak usage of electricity at night, the solar cells are not able to provide a supply. One answer is to use the battery in a battery electric car as a store. The solar cells can charge the battery during the day and at peak times, electricity can be extracted from the battery. (Discussed in *"Buying or Leasing a New Car"* chapter.) This does require a modification to the battery electric car but such systems are now available. This will help to resolve a problem of capacity of the electricity supply as more and more people switch to battery electric cars from petrol or diesel cars. (See *"Getting Further Information"* chapter)

Fully autonomous vehicles will obviate the need to drive at all, resulting in a true transport revolution. There are a few examples under development which demonstrate this potential technology. (See *"Getting Further Information"* chapter)

Whether the science fiction of hover cars will ever become reality, there is now considerable effort being put into the development of flying cars, often designed around scaled up drones. (See *"Getting Further Information"* chapter)

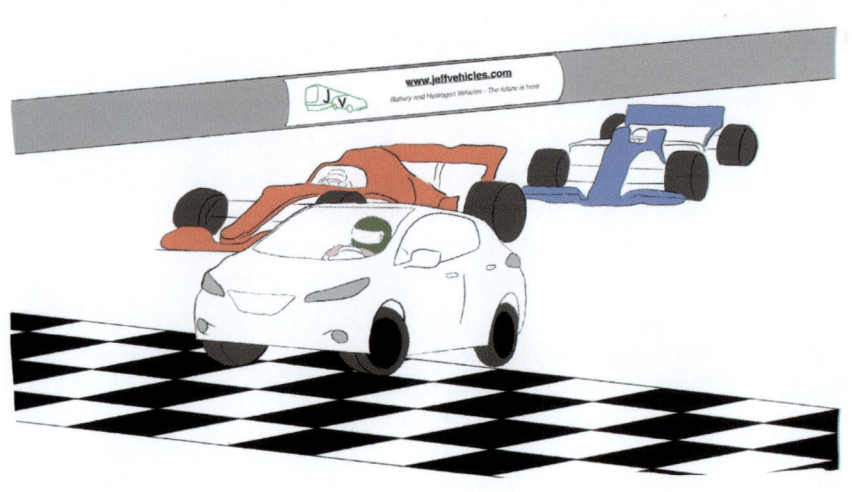

21 SPRINTS, HILLCLIMBS, SPEED TRIALS AND DRAG RACING

This may seem to be a strange chapter but drag racing is popular for those who have more powerful battery electric cars and I have successfully participated in amateur motor sport in the form of sprints, hillclimbs and speed trials. I am keen to have more competition. Unfortunately, no sprints, hillclimbs or speed trials took place in the UK between the 2017 and 2021 seasons due to the difficulty event organisers found in meeting the Motorsport UK's new safety requirements for events which include battery electric cars. In the 2021 season one hill climb at Shelsley Walsh took place and more venues are now available but progress is slow.

The aim of a sprint, hillclimb, or speed trial is to complete the course from a standing start in the shortest time possible. Each car is timed and competes with no other cars nearby. The car with the shortest time in their class wins. A hillclimb, as the name suggests, is typically a road with smooth tarmac (and of course no traffic) up a hill with bends to make the racing more exciting. A sprint takes place at a motor race course, such as Silverstone or Brands Hatch and typically consists of a lap of the course, or, occasionally two laps. A speed trial is a straight course typically

1/4 mile long. Drag racing is similar but with two cars running next to each other in parallel.

The advantage of sprints, hillclimbs and speed trials over more conventional motor racing is that you are not on track with other cars which could hit yours, you can use a conventional road car and the courses are short so the car is not unduly stressed.

You need safety equipment - a fireproof suit, a racing helmet and gloves and it is advisable to use fireproof shoes too. Very little is needed on the car; in essence, a timing strut to break a light beam at the start and finish, some numbers on the side of the car and tow hooks on back and front. You need to obtain a passport for your car from Motorsport UK. An electricity symbol is also required to indicate that it is not a conventional petrol /diesel car. (See *"Getting Further Information"* chapter).

Battery electric cars are well suited for these types of events. Initial acceleration is typically better than petrol car equivalents and the battery is low and heavy resulting in a low centre of gravity which is good for road handling.

At the beginning of an event, you have to register, producing your race licence. This is then followed by scrutineering where officials working for the event will check the safety of your car. The event starts with all cars completing two practice runs, one at a time. This is followed by two timed runs and an awards ceremony. It's an early start to the day but a finish which is around early evening. There is a lot of waiting between runs as it is not unusual to have around 100 cars competing. It is an excellent way of learning the full capabilities of your car.

Please search *"Electric Motorsports in UK"* on Facebook for support for drivers interested in competing in a battery electric car.

Preparing to be scrutineered

At the start line in the author's Tesla

22 GETTING FURTHER INFORMATION

1 Introduction

https://newautomotive.org/global-ev-tracker
This website shows how the UK is on track for car sales to be almost fully electric by 2030. Select "S Curve Like Adoption" in Data Set, select "UK" in Country Selector.

4 Economics

https://www.gov.uk/government/collections/government-grants-for-low-emission-vehicles
This website contains details on how to apply for a grant for a home charger for flats.

https://tfl.gov.uk/modes/driving/congestion-charge
This website shows how to get a discount for a battery electric car on the London congestion charge.

6 Safety

https://insideevs.com/news/630599/tesla-modely-models-euro-ncap-best-in-class/
This website states that two Tesla models made best in class in 2022 for NCAP ratings.

https://www.tesla.com/sites/default/files/downloads/2014-15 Dual Motor Model S Emergency Response Guide en.pdf
This website explains the special precautions the fire services need to apply to fires with battery electric cars including the need to monitor up to 24 hours after the fire has been put out.

7 Are You Saving the Planet?

https://www.withouthotair.com
This website gives access to the late Professor Sir David MacKay's free book "Sustainable Energy - without the hot air" which explains the carbon dioxide emissions for different forms of transport.

https://www.sciencedirect.com/science/article/pii/S1364032122000867
This website contains information on CO2 emissions as a result of car manufacturing - conventional petrol /diesel and battery electric.

http://electricityinfo.org/real-time-british-electricity -supply/
This website shows the current mix of sources of electricity generation in Britain so you can see how much is from renewable sources.

https://my2050.energysecurity.gov.uk/?levers=11111111111111
This website gives access to a tool whereby you can see the effects for Britain of changing electricity supply from coal to renewable energy, changing demand for transportation and the effect of changing over to a zero-carbon transport system. It was initially developed at the Department for Energy and Climate

Change (DECC) by Professor Sir David Mackay's team when he was chief scientific adviser to the government at DECC.

https://ourworldindata.org/energy #country-profiles
This website includes a breakdown of electricity sources by country.

http://www.greencarcongress.com/2012/06/harrison-20120611.html
This website describes the continuing health problem with cars due to tyre wear and brake dust, even when exhaust emissions are eliminated

https://www.electrive.com/2020/11/22/project-recovas-to-commercialise-battery -reuse-in-uk/
This website describes battery recycling processes for car batteries.

http://nissaninsider.co.uk/powering-ahead-with-second-life-battery -system/
This website explains how used battery electric car batteries can be used for a second life after they are no longer of use in a battery electric car.

https://www.gov.uk/government/publications/air-pollution-applying-all-our-health/air-pollution-applying-all-our-health#why-we-focus-on-the-health-effects-of-air-pollution-in-your-professional-practice
This website gives information on air pollution

https://www.gov.uk/government/statistics/reported-road-casualties-great-britain-annual-report-2023/reported-road-casualties-great-britain-annual-report-2023#headline-figures.
This website gives more information on deaths from road accidents as of 2023

8 Buying or Leasing a New Car

https://www.mg.co.uk/blog/vehicle-to-load-charging-v2l-guide
This website covers Vehicle to Load charging

https://pod-point.com/guides/vehicle-to-grid-v2g-explained
This website explains vehicle to grid – getting your car to power your house at night.

9 Buying a Used Car

https://www.tesla.com/en_GB/preowned
This website shows used Teslas for sale from the Tesla company.

https://usedcars.nissan.co.uk/en/nissan/leaf
This website shows used Nissan Leafs for sale from the Nissan company

http://eco-cars.net
This website specialises in selling used battery electric cars. It is one of the most established around.

http://www.autotrader.co.uk/used-cars/nissan/leaf
This website advertises used cars from dealers and private individuals.

https://greenmotion.co.uk/fleet
This website allows you to hire battery electric cars

https://www.mynissanleaf.com
This is a forum about Nissan Leafs.

http://www.mybmwi3.com
This is a forum about BMW i3s.

10 Charging at Home

https://www.gov.uk/government/collections/government-grants-for-low-emission-vehicles
This website contains details on how to apply for a grant for a home charger for flats.

https://www.gov.uk/government/collections/government-grants-for-low-emission-vehicles
This website contains details of how to apply for a grant for workplace chargers including eligibility.

https://www.ubitricity.com/en/
This website has details of street light charge points.

11 Travelling Long Distances

https://www.zap-map.com/live/
This website allows you to find and check the status of public charge points. You can get a phone app too.

https://www.plugshare.com
This website allows you to find and check the status of public charger charge points. You can get a phone app too.

https://www.gridserve.com/
This website allows you to register a phone app for Gridserve chargers, which are available extensively at English, Welsh, Norther Irish and Scottish motorway services.

12 Driving Abroad

https://shellrecharge.com/en-gb
This website allows you to register for a Shell Recharge app enabling you to use charging points in the UK - England, Wales, Scotland, Northern Ireland as well as: France, Germany, Belgium, Netherlands, Switzerland, Austria, Italy, Croatia, Czechia, Slovakia, Sweden, Norway, Albania, Macedonia, Romania and Russia. Please check carefully before you go that you have sufficient charge points on your route - Some countries only have a few charge points

https://www.esb.ie/our-businesses/ecars/charge-point-map
This website allows you to download a phone app to gain access to charge points in Ireland

https://www.amazon.co.uk or **https://www.ebay.co.uk**
Either of these two websites should enable you to buy a suitable adaptor to convert a European style domestic socket to a UK style plug. Search for "European plug to UK socket 13 amps". Ensure it has a European plug at one end, a cable, one or more UK sockets and most importantly, it is definitely rated at 13 amps.

https://www.theaa.com/european-breakdown-cover/driving-in-europe/what-do-i-need
This website gives information on what you need when driving in mainland Europe, over and above what is required in the UK.

14 Hydrogen Fuel Cell Cars

https://www.youtube.com/watch?v=lknzEAs34r0&t=1s
This video shows two cars being set alight - one a hydrogen car and the other a petrol car.

17 Battery Electric and Hydrogen Fuel Cell Trucks

https://ulemco.com/
This website describes the ULEMCo company and their products.

18 Converting Petrol Cars

https://www.retroelectrics.co.uk/
 https://www.electricclassiccars.co.uk
These are two websites offering information on converting petrol cars to battery electric.

https://www.everything-ev.com/index.php
This website provides a list of suppliers in the UK for these components

19 History

https://brightonmuseums.org.uk/brighton/
This website gives further information on the Museum and Art Gallery which has all manner of objects and information associated with Brighton, not least photographs of Magnus Volk and his inventions.

http://www.whokilledtheelectriccar.com
This website gives details of the documentary produced by Chris Paine. The DVD is available from **www.amazon.co.uk** or iTunes.

20 Future Trends

https://interestingengineering.com/science/could-ultracapacitors-replace-batteries-in-future-electric-vehicles
This website has a short article on the possible future of supercapacitors.

https://www.zipcar.com/en-gb/car-hire-london
This website describes a means of hiring a car in London simply by using the app near the hire car.

https://pod-point.com/guides/vehicle-to-grid -v2g-explained
This website has an article on vehicle to grid technology whereby electric cars are used to stabilise an electricity network.

https://www.mckinsey.com/industries/automotive-and-assembly /our-insights/autonomous-drivings-future-convenient-and-connected
This website describes the progression of autonomous cars from the perspective of car manufacturers.

https://www.techradar.com/news/flying-car-watch-as-this-drone-flies-around-with-passengers-inside
This website includes a video of a drone based flying car.

21 Sprints, Hillclimbs, Speed Trials and Drag racing

https://www.motorsportuk.org
This website gives information on Motorsport UK which is the governing body for amateur motor sports in the UK. It is where to apply for a race licence and passport. It also has information about safety equipment needed

INDEX

20

History of electric vehicles, 72–75
Home charging, 39–45
Hybrid cars, 53–55
Hydrogen Fuel Cell Cars, 56–59

I
Insurance, 12
Introduction, 1–2

K
Kerbocharge, 43
Kia, 55

L
Lamp post chargers, 44
Leasing, 11–13, 24
LEZ/CAZ (Low Emission/Clean Air Zones), 13
Lifetime considerations, 14–16
Low mileage concerns, 35–36

M
Material resources, 22–23
MG, 31–32
Micro hybrids, 54
MOT, 12

N
Nissan Leaf, 36

O
Operating costs, 11–13

P
Parking etiquette (charging), 48
Petrol vs electric comparison, 11–13, 19–23
Plug-in hybrids, 53–55
Polestar, 29
Portable chargers, 42

R
Range – considerations, 6–10, 24–26, 33–34
Range – winter/summer variation, 5, 24
Recycling – batteries and cars, 22–23
Regenerative braking, 4, 15–16

S
Safety – electric vehicles, 17–18
Servicing, 12
Solar panels – home use, 23
Speed limits, 27
Sprints, hill climbs, etc., 78–80
Stop-start (micro hybrids), 54
Sustainable transport alternatives, 19

T
Tesla, 4, 11–12, 26–27, 34–35, 47–50
Trials – user experience, 24–25, 33–35
Tyre wear, 15–16, 22

U
ULEMCo, 68
Used cars, 33–38

V
Vehicle to Grid (V2G), 30
Vehicle to Load (V2L), 30
Volkswagen, 29

W
Warranty, 33
Winter driving, 5, 24, 36

Z
Zap Map app, 46–51

ABOUT THE AUTHOR AND ILLUSTRATOR

Jeff Allan

Professor Jeff Allan is an award-winning chartered engineer who runs Jeff Vehicles Ltd., promoting battery electric and hydrogen solutions for road and rail vehicles. (**www.jeffvehicles.com**). He competes in amateur motorsport - speed trials, sprints and hillclimbs in battery electric cars. He has won the Brighton national speed trials, battery electric car class twice. He jointly holds two Guinness World Records with his son for shortest charging time of a battery electric car from John o'Groats to Land's End and shortest charging time for a battery electric car across Europe (Nordkapp, Norway to Tarifa, Spain). He is on his fourth battery electric car, having started using one in 2010.

He was born in New York and lives in Birmingham. His Ph.D., completed in 1981 was concerned with regenerative braking and he has 50 years of experience working on electric railways. He is a consultant on innovation in railways. He helped design the first and second hydrogen powered trains in the U.K. He is currently working on the first UK hydrogen shunting locomotive He has had a lifelong interest in cars. He built one when he was 17 years old

Maddie Cottam-Allan.

Maddie Cottam-Allan is a professional artist, comic writer/illustrator and photographer. She regularly posts her comics and illustrations to her Instagram **@maddiecottamallan** and her photos on **@maddiecottamallanphotos**. Maddie is the artist behind the Birmingham tap water merchandise which can be obtained from her Instagram account. She studied at the Birmingham School of Art.

Printed in Dunstable, United Kingdom

64808106R00056